T0380240

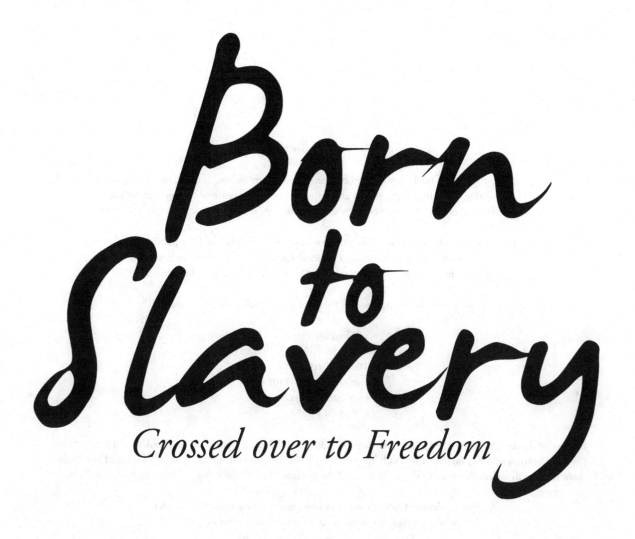

Born to Slavery

Crossed over to Freedom

JENNIFER JAMES LEWIS

WestBow
PRESS®
A DIVISION OF THOMAS NELSON
& ZONDERVAN

Copyright © 2020 Jennifer James Lewis.

All rights reserved. No part of this book may be used or reproduced by any means, graphic, electronic, or mechanical, including photocopying, recording, taping or by any information storage retrieval system without the written permission of the author except in the case of brief quotations embodied in critical articles and reviews.

This book is a work of non-fiction. Unless otherwise noted, the author and the publisher make no explicit guarantees as to the accuracy of the information contained in this book and in some cases, names of people and places have been altered to protect their privacy.

WestBow Press books may be ordered through booksellers or by contacting:

WestBow Press
A Division of Thomas Nelson & Zondervan
1663 Liberty Drive
Bloomington, IN 47403
www.westbowpress.com
844-714-3454

Because of the dynamic nature of the Internet, any web addresses or links contained in this book may have changed since publication and may no longer be valid. The views expressed in this work are solely those of the author and do not necessarily reflect the views of the publisher, and the publisher hereby disclaims any responsibility for them.

Any people depicted in stock imagery provided by Getty Images are models, and such images are being used for illustrative purposes only.
Certain stock imagery © Getty Images.

Scriptures taken from the Holy Bible, New International Version®, NIV®. Copyright © 1973, 1978, 1984, 2011 by Biblica, Inc.™ Used by permission of Zondervan. All rights reserved worldwide. www.zondervan.com The "NIV" and "New International Version" are trademarks registered in the United States Patent and Trademark Office by Biblica, Inc.®

ISBN: 978-1-6642-1208-4 (sc)
ISBN: 978-1-6642-1209-1 (e)

Library of Congress Control Number: 2020922261

Print information available on the last page.

WestBow Press rev. date: 11/17/2020

This book is dedicated to God because he gave me the confidence and strength to write it. Hebrews 11:1 (NIV) tells us, "Faith is confidence in what we hope for and assurance about what we do not see. That is what the ancients were commended for."

I dedicate this book also to my husband, who always encouraged me to not quit, and my mother, Gwen James, and father, Walter James, who encouraged me all through my life to pursue my dreams.

PROLOGUE

Promise, from New Orleans, was born into slavery. This is her story.

She was lying in bed with her grandchildren, daughters, and son. Her daughters, Serenity and Rachel, were holding her hands. Her granddaughter, Prayer, and her son, David Jr., were on her left.

Serenity hugged her and said, "I love you, Mommy. You and Daddy gave our family such a good life."

Promise sat up and looked at everyone around the bed. "God has been so good to me. He allowed me to be free. My mommy's desire was to see me free. If only Joseph could have lived to see all of you children."

She had tears in her eyes. She told Prayer, "Give me Joseph's picture."

His picture was on the dresser. Prayer handed the picture to Promise, who held it close to her heart. Promise said, "I love this man. He had the heart to do the Lord's work. I loved him very much. I want to tell you the story of how God freed me and how I loved your father. The story starts off with your great-grandmother Sarah. Charles, her husband, did work in the house. He was a light-skinned man, and he loved Sarah. Here's my story."

Chapter

1

The master was John Winston, and his wife was Virginia, who was three months pregnant and had been married for only a year when John was killed in a wagon accident. Virginia had the baby, Joseph, but she had a hard time giving birth to him. The doctor told her that if she got pregnant again, it would kill her.

Virginia remarried a year later to Master Avery Jones, who raised Joseph like his own. Virginia loved children and was always so kind to them. It did not matter if they were black—she loved on all the children. A lot of what she did was in private. The law could kill you if they knew you were showing kindness to blacks.

The master had a big house, many businesses, and a cotton field, and he ran Friendship Baptist Church. Virginia taught my mother, Sarah, to read the Bible, and she also taught Charles how to read. She was nothing like Master Jones, who was always drinking and yelling at her; he called her names that made her cry. Virginia loved her husband and always prayed for him. At church, he would preach the Bible.

Sarah was a beautiful woman with long black hair, light skin, and green eyes. She could pass as a white woman, but she was black. She had a beautiful voice and would sing when she could, mostly around her house. Her favorite song was "Wade in the Water." She loved reading the Bible.

At night before going to sleep, Sarah and Charles would pray before bed. Sarah said that prayer was very important.

Charles would help Master Jones in the house. My mother and her sister, Mary, worked very hard in the house. Sarah's dream was to have children. They would try, but Sarah never got pregnant. However, she never gave up. She said to Charles in the cabin once, "I will have a child one day."

The master would bring Sarah and Charles to church, and they loved that. They would sit up front and assist the people in church. Virginia would come down where the slaves were and would read the Bible. The master stayed in the house. Virginia would talk about Jesus Christ to the slaves, and some slaves would shout and even be baptized. She was a good woman, but the master was mean to her. There were rumors that he ran around with other women, but Virginia was loyal to Master Jones and stood by his side.

At church, Sarah would see the master looking at her, so one day, Sarah asked, "Master, do you need something?"

Master said, "You look nice." He winked at Sarah, who later told Charles, "Master was looking at me funny."

"How did he look at you?" he asked.

"He winked at me."

"Be careful," he said and took her hand.

"I will."

One day, Virginia was gone for the day and Sarah was cleaning the den. Master came in with a bottle in his hand. She asked him, "Are you okay?"

Master tried to kiss her. Sarah ran from him toward the door, but it was closed. Master Jones threw her on the couch. As Sarah got up, he pushed her to the floor and ripped her dress. Sarah screamed, but Master Jones raped her. When Master Jones was done, he pulled up his pants and walked out of the den. Mary came into the room. She saw him leave the room as Sarah lay on the floor crying. Mary helped Sarah back to her cabin. Charles was there cooking, and when he saw Sarah, he asked, "What happened?"

"Master had his way with me!" she cried out.

"I heard a lot of noise and screams," Mary said.

"I'll hurt him!" Charles said.

Mary grabbed Charles. "No! Don't! I know you're upset, but you'll get yourself killed. Plus, Sarah needs you."

Charles hugged Sarah and helped her get into bed.

After that incident, Sarah became jumpy. The master would get drunk and wait for Virginia to leave the house. Then he would call for Sarah, throw her on the floor, and rape her. After a few months, Sarah found herself throwing up in the morning. She found out she was pregnant.

Sarah told Charles, "I'm with child."

Charles looked at Sarah with a tear in his eye and said, "It's your fault. Why?" He ran off.

Sarah told Mary, "I am with child."

Mary held Sarah and said, "I'll help you."

Sarah told Mary, "Charles blames me. This was not supposed to happen this way!"

Mary just held Sarah.

One day, Sarah had a rope in one hand and a Bible in the other. She looked to the sky and said, "Forgive me for what I am about to do. I have nothing to live for." She was putting the rope around her neck when she felt it was not right. She sat by the tree and cried. She said, "What do I do? I'm pregnant with the master's child." She opened her Bible to John 10:10: "The thief comes only to steal and kill and destroy. I have come that they may have life and have it to the full." Sarah fainted, and when she came around, Virginia was over her.

"What happened, Sarah? Are you okay? What are you doing with that rope?"

Sarah said, "Nothing. I'm okay."

Virginia helped Sarah to her cabin, where Mary helped her to bed.

Later the same day, Charles came in and said, "Forgive me for what I said. I love you. We'll deal with this."

Sarah hugged him and cried.

Sarah kept working in the house. As her stomach got bigger, she told Mary that she had dreams that her child would be free. Mary said, "That won't happen." But Sarah knew in her spirit that one day it would happen; she knew the baby she was carrying would be free.

Virginia saw Sarah and said, "So you are with child. I see you're getting bigger. I bet you and Charles are happy."

Sarah said, "Yes, I'm finally with child."

Later, Sarah told Charles, "I have never lied to Virginia. I told her we are with child."

Charles hugged her. He asked her what she wanted to name the baby.

Sarah said, "I don't know. I feel guilty about lying to Virginia."

The master was at the door, and he heard Sarah and Charles talking. He walked into the den, where Virginia was seated at a desk. He told Virginia, "I've decided to sell Charles."

"Why? He's a good worker—"

Master Jones interrupted her. "That's my final decision."

The next morning, Sarah was washing dishes in the big house. Virginia said, "Sarah, sit down. I have something to tell you. Charles will be sold. I tried to talk my husband out of that, but he won't listen."

With tears in her eyes, Sarah said, "Please no! I have something to tell you. Charles is not the father. Master Jones is. He had his way with me."

"What?" Virginia asked.

"He had his way with me. I'm sorry. It was my fault."

"No, it's not your fault," Virginia said and hugged Sarah.

Later that day, Virginia told Master Jones, "You were with another woman!"

"What are you talking about?" he asked.

"I know you were with Sarah, and she's carrying your child. You wanted to sell Charles off when you found out."

Master Jones threw a vase across the room. "I'll do what I want and sell whom I want!"

The next day, Charles was to be sold. Master Jones told Charles, "Come on!"

Sarah and Charles hugged. She cried when Charles got into the wagon and left with Master Jones.

Chapter

A few months later, Sarah was in the cabin cleaning. Virginia walked in and saw Sarah crying. Virginia hugged her, and Sarah said, "I miss Charles. I love him!"

Virginia said, "I know. I'm trying to find out where Charles is. Master Jones has the information in a book, but I don't know where it is."

Sarah started bleeding and was crying. Virginia helped her to the bed. Sarah said, "It hurts!" She started huffing and puffing. "Go get Mary!"

Virginia ran to get Mary, and they were helping Sarah deliver her baby. At one point, Sarah said, "This is it!" She pushed, and the baby came out and started crying.

Mary said, "It's a girl!" She gave the baby to Sarah, who looked at the newborn and said, "I'll name her Promise because I knew in my spirit she will be free."

There was a lot of blood on the floor. Virginia told Mary, "She looks weak."

Sarah said, "She's so beautiful," and handed Promise to Virginia. Sarah said, "You're a good woman, and you have been very kind to me. Please watch over my baby." With tears in her eyes, she said, "I won't be around to see her grow up. Mary, I love you. Teach my child. Watch over her."

Sarah looked at Virginia holding the baby and she shook and closed her eyes. Mary screamed, held onto Sarah, and cried. Virginia and Mary put a sheet over Sarah. Virginia said, "I'll raise Promise in the house."

"What about Master Jones?" Mary asked.

"I'll handle him."

Virginia took the baby to the house; Master Jones was eating dinner. Virginia said, "Here's your daughter from Sarah."

Master Jones looked shocked. "Where's Sarah?"

"She died after the baby was born."

After looking at Virginia and the baby, he left the room.

Virginia told Promise, "I'll look after you and raise you here right along with Joseph."

The next day, Sarah was buried in the field. Virginia read Psalm 23 and said, "That scripture was Sarah's favorite."

Mary was holding the baby. Virginia sang "Wade in the Water."

Chapter

Promise was raised in the house. Ten years later, she was two years younger than Joseph.

One day, Promise, who was light skinned and had long hair with two braids, was wearing a pink dress. She and Joseph were running and playing on the front porch as Virginia was on the porch, too, reading the Bible.

Master Jones came on the porch and said, "Promise, go to your room. I have to talk with your mother and Joseph."

Promise asked, "Do I have to?"

He said yes, and Promise went to her room upstairs.

Master Jones said to Virginia and Joseph, "She can play with Joseph at the house but not in public."

Joseph asked, "Why not? She's my sister!"

"She is not!" Master Jones said.

Joseph said, "But she's my friend!"

Master Jones yelled, "I have the final word!" and walked into the house.

Joseph hugged Virginia and cried.

A few minutes later, Promise came outside with tears in her eyes. Virginia said, "You heard," and Promise nodded. She hugged Virginia.

Joseph asked his mother, "Why is Daddy so mean?"

Virginia said, "We have to continue to pray for him, Joseph. He's your father."

Joseph said, "I know, but he yells at you, Mommy, and he's mean to you and is always yelling at you. I don't like it!"

Virginia said, "I know," and she hugged the children.

Master Jones would take Joseph to his friends' houses and on outings, but Promise had to stay home. She went to church with Virginia and Joseph, but if the church was hosting a picnic or gathering, she had to stay home.

When it was Joseph's thirteenth birthday, there was big party, but Promise could not come out of her room. She looked out the window with tears in her eyes and saw the other children having a good time. Mary came in with a piece of cake for the girl, and Promise asked, "Why does Master Jones hate me?"

Mary said, "He doesn't, but there are rules you have to follow."

After everyone had left, Promise gave Joseph a card she had made and said, "Happy birthday!"

Joseph hugged her and said, "I love your card. I wished my father had let you come down to the birthday party."

The next night, Promise could not sleep and decided to step out onto the porch. It was a warm night with a full moon. She sat and started reading her Bible. She saw a woman wearing a shiny dress standing by the door and smiling. The woman touched her, and Promise fell.

The next thing she knew, Virginia and Master Jones were asking her, "Are you okay?"

Virginia said, "I saw you on the floor with tears in your eyes."

Master Jones walked back to his bedroom. Virginia helped Promise to her room and back to bed. After Virginia left, Promise got out of bed and looked out the window. She said, "Yes, I will."

The next night, Joseph saw a smiling woman wearing a shiny white gown and holding a Bible. She touched Joseph, who fainted.

When he came to, Virginia was over him asking if he was okay. She helped him back to bed and read the Bible to him. Joseph fell back to sleep.

Chapter

Joseph and Promise were at church with Virginia and Master Jones. Master Jones had just finished preaching, and a blind woman walked up with help from a woman and said, "I need prayer."

Virginia started to pray with the woman. Then Master Jones started praying. Joseph was sitting on the bench. Virginia called Promise up and asked her to pray for the woman.

Promise started praying for her and saw scales falling off her eyes. The blind woman yelled and opened her eyes and said, "I can see! This is a miracle!"

After the service, the blind woman told Promise, "Thank you! Your prayer made a difference. I can see, and I haven't been able to see since I was child. I was stricken with a bad case of the flu and went blind. I was given back my sight. Thank you!"

Promise smiled.

Master Jones told her, "You did a good thing today," and walked away.

Promise told Virginia, "Wow! Jesus does miracles."

Later that day, Virginia said to Promise and Joseph, "I want you both to conduct the service tonight at the slaves' cabin."

Joseph asked, "What's wrong, Mother? Are you okay?"

She said, "I'm just a little tired tonight. You two do the service."

Promise said, "Okay," and they went to conduct the service. Joseph preached the Bible, and those there were crying and shouting.

After the service, Joseph and Promise told Virginia about it. Virginia said, "I'm proud of both of you. You two keep reading the Bible. Remember to keep the Word in your heart."

Promise asked, "Are you okay? You don't look good."

Virginia took Promise's hand. "I'm okay, just a little tired. Go to sleep."

Promise hugged Virginia, and Joseph kissed her forehead.

Promise could not sleep that night, so she went to Mary's cabin.

"Promise, what are you doing down here?" Mary asked.

Promise said, "I couldn't sleep."

Mary started to walk to the table but almost fell. Promise caught her and helped her to her bed. "What's wrong?"

"My body hurts all over. I'm hot, and I can barely walk," Mary said.

Promise put Mary's Bible on her chest and said a prayer. The power of God came in, and Mary got up and shouted, "I'm healed!" She hugged Promise and said, "Thank you for the prayer! I feel so much better."

Mary went back to bed and fell asleep. Promise sat with her till morning, when Mary got up and made Promise a nice breakfast. She hugged Promise with tears in her eyes. "You're doing the Lord's work, Promise!"

Chapter

One day, Virginia was walking and heard laughter coming from the barn, which was right behind the church. The barn door was open, and Virginia walked in and saw Master Jones kissing a woman. "What is this?" Virginia asked.

The two looked at Virginia, and the woman ran out of the barn. Virginia asked, "What are you doing? This is it! You run around with other women. You drink and want me to cover up your sin. You are not father to Joseph or Promise. I am leaving you and taking Joseph and Promise."

Master Jones said, "Oh really? Where would you go? I have all the money. I'll tell the sheriff. You know what they will do to you!" He smiled.

"I'll take the children, and you'll never find me!"

He slapped Virginia, who fell. He put his hands on her neck and said, "You will stay as my wife and the mother of my children and be a loving, supporting wife and pillar of the church and community!"

She slapped him, and he started hitting her. Then he kissed her and raped her. When he was finished, he got up, grabbed his bottle of brandy, and walked out of the barn.

Virginia's clothes were ripped, and blood was coming from her mouth. She stood but fell. She got up again and walked into the church all the way to the altar. She fell down and cried out, "Jesus!" She started praying and prayed all night.

In the morning, Joseph walked in and saw her on the floor. He helped her up and asked, "What happened to you? You didn't come home last night. Your face looks beat up, and your clothes are ripped. Master Jones is worried about you."

"I'm okay. I just prayed all night."

"Mom, aren't you going to tell me what happened?"

Virginia looked away and got up.

Master Jones came in and asked, "Darling, where have you been? I've been worried!" He hugged her and said, "Let's go back to the house." He told Joseph, "Your mother will be fine."

Master Jones helped her into the wagon and drove to the house. When Promise saw Virginia come in with Master Jones, she asked, "Where have you been? Your clothes and face! What happened?"

Master Jones said, "She'll be okay, Promise. Mary, help Virginia to bed."

Mary helped Virginia to her bedroom, cleaned her up, and helped her to bed. After Mary left, Virginia started crying.

Promise walked into her bedroom and sat on the bed. Promise was crying. She asked, "What happened to you?" Virginia hugged her and cried. Promise sat with Virginia until she fell asleep.

Later on that night, Promise was looking out her window. She asked, "God, what's going on with Virginia?"

Joseph walked into her room and asked, "Did Mother tell you anything?"

"No."

Joseph said, "She's not telling me the truth."

Promise took Joseph's hand and said, "Let's pray for her."

Chapter

On the morning of Promise's sixteenth birthday, she heard a knock on the door. "Come in."

Mary came in and said, "Happy birthday!" She hugged Promise and gave her a package. "Open it, Promise!"

Promise opened the package; it was a blanket. She hugged Mary and said, "Thank you!"

"I knitted this for you."

"It's beautiful!" Promise said and hugged Mary again.

Later on that day, Promise sat down for breakfast. She was wearing a purple dress, and her hair was up in a bun. Virginia brought Promise a box and said, "Happy birthday!" and kissed her forehead. Promise smiled and open the box; in it was a gold necklace and a locket. Virginia told Promise to open it, and Promise did. Virginia said, "This is a picture of your mother." Virginia had tears in her eyes. "You look like your mother. I miss her. She was a sweet woman who loved you and wanted the best for you."

She took Promise's hand. "I raised you, and I love you. I want you to know the truth."

Promise hugged Virginia. "I love you too. Thank you for giving me good life."

Promise put on the necklace, and Virginia said, "I will tell you about your mommy. Your mom worked for me and Master Jones, and she had husband named Charles. Master Jones found out about your mother being pregnant and sold Charles. I don't know where he is. Master Jones has the information in a book, but I don't know where it is. You're getting older, and I wanted you to know the truth."

Promise said, "I always knew there was something different about me. Master Jones doesn't really care about me." She started crying. "I'll never stop praying for him. I've heard the people in the house who work for you talking." Promise hugged Virginia again. "You're a sweet woman."

Later that day, Promise was sitting in a tree. Joseph climbed up, put a package in her lap, and said, "Happy birthday!"

Promise opened the package, which contained a shawl. "Thank you. I love it."

Joseph asked, "What's wrong?"

"Your mother told me about my mother." Promise hugged Joseph.

"How do you feel about it?"

"I'm shocked, but I knew the truth deep down. Mary talked to me when I was younger, but I was trying to ignore the truth."

Joseph told Promise that Master Jones was not his father, that his father had been killed in a wagon accident before he was born. Promise looked at Joseph with tears in his eyes. Joseph said, "Even though I didn't know him, I felt that he loved me."

Joseph walked Promise back to her room and hugged her. He said, "You look beautiful!" and kissed her cheek. Joseph looked at Promise, and Promise and Joseph shared a kiss. Promise said goodnight to him and went into her room.

Later on that night, Promise could not sleep and looked out the window with a prayer. "God, I liked the kiss, but I must stay focused on what you called me to do—heal the sick."

While Promise was asleep, Master Jones came into her room, left a wrapped package on her nightstand, and left.

When Promise woke up, she saw the package and opened it; it was a book. Promise knew in her spirit that Master Jones had given it to her. Later, when she saw him in the kitchen, she thanked him, and he said, "You're welcome."

Later on that morning, Promise saw Joseph on the porch and told him, "The kiss cannot happen again."

"Why not?" he asked.

"I'm set aside for the Lord's work, healing the sick. You have been called too. We cannot—"

Joseph said, "I like you and your spirit."

Promise said, "I can't do this."

She walked into the house and saw Master Jones as she went to her room.

Master Jones said to Joseph, "You kissed her."

"Mind your own business," Joseph said.

"You are never to kiss her again. That isn't proper. You can have any other girl you want but not her." Master Jones got into Joseph's face. "Understand?"

Joseph ran into the house.

Chapter

One Sunday, when Promise, Master Jones, Virginia, and Joseph were at church, a man walked up to Master Jones and said, "My name is John. The town officials have looked at you. You're highly respected, and you would be a good mayor for New Orleans."

Master Jones said, "I don't know, but this is an honor."

John said, "Some of the officials would like to discuss this with you."

Master Jones said, "Of course. Why don't you come tonight for dinner? We would love to have you."

After John left, Master Jones said, "Well, that would be an honor. Virginia, I expect you to be by my side with Joseph. Promise, you will have dinner in your room."

That evening, John and two others came for dinner and to discuss Master Jones's being the mayor. After they left, Virginia went to Promise's room and told her, "It's official. Master Jones will be running for mayor."

Promise asked, "How do you feel about this?"

Virginia said, "I don't know, but I'll stay in prayer about it."

The next day, Master Jones came limping onto the porch, where Virginia and Promise were sitting. He said, "I tripped on a rock in the cotton field. This hurts so bad!" He sat and took off his boot. Promise put her hand on his red foot and said a prayer. The redness went away. He stood and walked on it and told Promise, "I really thank you. I feel better."

Virginia smiled at Promise.

In a few months, Master Jones was elected mayor, and a big party was given in his honor, but Promise had to stay in her room. At the party, Master Jones told Joseph, "I want you to meet Sally, a councilman's daughter. Show her a good time."

Sally, who had blonde hair and was wearing a long green-and-white dress, said, "I'm very glad to meet you."

Joseph said, "Glad to meet you too."

Master Jones said, "Son, why don't you dance with her."

Joseph and Sally did dance, and Sally said, "You dance well."

Joseph said, "Thank you."

Sally said, "Let's get some punch and get to know each other." She grabbed his arm and led him to the punch bowl.

Promise was in her room reading the Bible when she heard a knock. She opened the door and saw Joseph, who said, "I just had to get away from that party."

"It sounded like you were having a good time," Promise said.

"My father introduced me to another girl, Sally. She's nice, but I'm not interested in her. I'm interested in someone else. You."

Master Jones was listening behind Promise's door.

Joseph took Promise's hand and looked into her eyes.

Promise was teary eyed. "I can't. Our lives would be affected, and I've been called to do the Lord's work."

"Promise, I'd never interrupt the Lord's work. I see how the Lord uses you."

"We can't be together. We both have been called. I have to go and see Mary."

Master Jones heard that and quickly went downstairs before Promise walked out.

After the party, Master Jones told Joseph, "Son, I saw you with Sally. She's beautiful."

Joseph said, "She is lovely."

"I want you to start courting her."

"What? I don't like her in that way."

"It seems she likes you."

"No, Father. I—"

"You'll do what I say. Do you want me to sell Promise? I don't have to keep her."

"You wouldn't!" Joseph said.

"Yes I would. She's beautiful. I could sell her for a lot."

Joseph raced out of the house and saw Virginia on the porch; he told her what his father was threatening to do if he did not start courting Sally, and she said that she would talk to him.

Later, Virginia told Master Jones, "I talked to your son, and he told me what you said about dating Sally."

"They'll make a nice couple."

"But Joseph isn't interested in her."

He got in Virginia's face. "He'll do what I told him to do, and you'll listen to your husband!" He grabbed a bottle of brandy and went out the door.

On Sunday morning, Master Jones told Promise, "You'll not be going to church with us anymore. Starting today, you'll work in the house with Mary and live in her slave cabin."

Promise said, "But—"

Master Jones said, "You'll do what I say! Virginia will not stop me. You and Joseph can still preach to the help."

Master Jones walked away. When Promise started to cry, Mary hugged her and started praying.

JENNIFER JAMES LEWIS

Chapter

When Promise was in Mary's cabin getting ready to preach that evening, Virginia came, gave her a hug, and said, "Master Jones told me and Joseph of what was done. We tried to talk to him, but he won't change his mind."

Promise said, "It's okay. I'm all right. I did a lot of crying. I don't understand God's will, but I accept it."

"I love you, Promise, as if you were my daughter. I also love Joseph. He told me what Master Jones told him he must do to keep you from being sold. Joseph said he would do it."

Promise said, "No!"

Joseph knocked and came in the cabin; he hugged Promise and told her, "I'll do what it takes to keep you from being sold. Mother, what are we going to do?"

"I don't know, but we'll pray and trust in God. Promise, I see how you two look at each other. Joseph doesn't love Sally. He loves you."

Promise said, "I can't do this! It doesn't matter how I feel. I must do the Lord's work."

Virginia asked, "Do you love Joseph?"

"Yes, but we'll all die if this comes out."

"I want both of you to be happy. We'll pray about this, and God will work it out. Promise, tonight, you'll give the service."

That night, Promise preached a powerful sermon on trusting God even if you were in pain and didn't understand your situation. Many people gave their lives to Christ that night.

After the service, Virginia told Joseph and Promise, "God will work this situation out for his glory," and walked back to the house.

Joseph held Promise's hand and looked into her eyes. "I love you. You have such a sweet spirit."

Promise hugged him. "I love you too."

They walked to Mary's cabin, and Joseph said, "Good night," kissed her hand, and left.

In the cabin, Mary told Promise, "That was good preaching. I worry about you. I don't want to see you killed."

Promise said, "God will work it out."

The next night, Mary woke up Promise and said, "Come to Grace's cabin. Her son has a high fever."

The two got there, and Grace told Promise, "There's nothing you can't do."

Promise put her Bible on the sick child lying in bed and started praying. All of a sudden, the boy opened his eyes and looked at his mom. The mother started crying and told Promise, "Thank you! You gave my son back to me!" They all hugged.

The next day, Promise was dusting in the living room when Master Jones walked in with a young man. He said, "This is Matthew. He'll be working in the house. I bought him today. You show him his duties."

Matthew was tall, light skinned, and blue eyed. He said, "Glad to meet you."

Promise showed Matthew around the house and explained his duties.

When Promise's workday was over, she was sitting at the kitchen table when Master Jones walked up and said, "The house looks very nice. You know how to keep a house."

Promise said, "Thank you."

"I want you to be nice to Matthew and teach him what he needs to know."

"Yes sir, Master Jones."

Later that evening, Promise read her Bible in the cabin and then walked out to the porch. She was looking at the moon when Joseph walked up. "You look beautiful tonight," he said.

Promise took Joseph by the hand and went into the cabin. Mary was asleep in the bedroom. Promise told Joseph what Master Jones had said to her about Matthew. Joseph said, "My father is going to be watching us." He took Promise's hand and said, "God will work this out."

Promise hugged Joseph.

Chapter

One day when Virginia was looking in the den for some paper to write a letter, she found a book under the desk. She looked in it and saw Charles's name. She learned that he had been sold to Mr. Jenkins, who was only down the road. Virginia put her hand over her mouth.

Master Jones walked in and saw Virginia reading the book. He said, "You just couldn't mind your own business, could you?"

Virginia said, "I didn't see anything!"

He shut the den door and started yelling at and hitting Virginia, who hit her head on the desk. He took a bottle of brandy and walked out.

A few minutes later, Mary walked into the den and saw a bloody Virginia on the floor and not moving. She got Matthew to help her get Virginia to her room. Mary called out, "Virginia's hurt!"

Joseph ran to his mother's room and asked Mary, "What happened?"

"I don't know. I heard yelling in the den, and after Master Jones left the room, I went in and saw her all bloody on the floor."

Joseph said, "Find Master Jones and get Promise."

Mary ran to get Promise, who was in the kitchen, and told her what had happened. Promise ran to Virginia and held her hand; she started praying.

Joseph said, "Matthew, go with Mary to get the doctor."

The doctor came and examined Virginia. He said, "I gave her shot to help the pain."

Promise asked, "Will she be okay?"

The doctor said, "I don't know, but I'll be back tomorrow to check on her."

Promise started to cry. Joseph held her and said, "She'll be okay. Promise, go get some rest."

"I can't leave her," she said.

"I'll stay with Mother," he said.

Mary led Promise from the room, and Matthew came in and told Joseph, "I looked all over the property but didn't find Master Jones."

Joseph sat next to the bed and fell asleep.

Two hours later, Master Jones walked into the bedroom and asked, "What happened?"

Joseph woke up and said, "I didn't know where you were."

"I was downtown having a meeting with the council."

"Liar! You've been drinking!"

"No! I love your mama!" He took her hand. "I'll find out who did this."

Mary came into Virginia's room and said, "I'll make some tea." She left.

Joseph said to Master Jones, "I'll find out who did this."

The next day, the doctor examined Virginia and told Master Jones and Joseph, "It doesn't look good, but she's stable. Let me know when she wakes up." He left the house.

Master Jones told Joseph, "Go get Promise."

Joseph left, and Master Jones was alone in the bedroom with Virginia. He said, "Darling, I'm so sorry. This was my fault." He had tears in his eyes. He took her hand. "Come back to me. I love you!"

Joseph went to the cabin and told Promise, "Come and pray for Virginia."

As Promise and Joseph went to the house, Sally came up and hugged Joseph. "I heard about your mama. I'm so sorry."

Joseph thanked her.

When Promise entered Virginia's room, Master Jones hugged her and said, "Please bring her back!" Promise hugged Master Jones and started praying with Joseph. When Virginia opened her eyes, Promise started to cry. Master Jones said, "Darling!" with tears in his eyes.

Virginia said, "Promise, keep doing God's work. I won't be here much longer. Keep doing the Lord's work. You were chosen, and you will be free. Joseph, keep doing the Lord's work too. I leave you my mantle." She looked at Master Jones and took his hand. "I will always love you."

"I was so mad at you," Master Jones said. "I love you."

Virginia looked at everyone with tears in her eyes and said, "I love all of you." She shook and closed her eyes. Promise, Joseph, and Master Jones were crying as Master Jones pulled the sheet over Virginia.

Chapter

Master Jones asked Promise to sing at Virginia's funeral. The church was packed. Promise sang "Wade in the Water," Virginia's favorite song. Everybody in the church clapped when Promise finished.

Master Jones conducted the service. Joseph sat up front, and Sally sat behind him. After the service, everybody went back to the house. Master Jones went straight to the den and shut the door. Mary and Matthew were busy serving the people, and Promise helped them. She did not see Joseph anywhere in the house, so she walked to the oak tree on the property and saw him sitting under it.

Joseph told Promise, "I miss her."

Promise hugged him and said, "I blamed myself. I thought she would live when she woke up, but she died."

Joseph said, "It's not your fault. She loved you and always talked about you." He hugged Promise, and when Sally saw that from a distance, she ran to the porch in tears.

Master Jones saw her and asked, "What's wrong?"

"Joseph doesn't love me. He loves Promise."

"Oh no. He loves you."

"I love him and would do anything for him."

"I'll talk to Joseph and straighten this out."

The next day, Joseph entered the den and told his father, "Mary said you wanted to talk to me."

Master Jones said, "Your mommy's death was a sad event. This house needs some joy in it. You've been courting Sally for a year. Don't you think you should get engaged?"

"I'm not ready yet."

"Sure you are. You'll propose to Sally or else I'll sell Promise."

"You never change!" Joseph said and left the house.

Promise was washing clothes when Matthew walked up to her and said, "You look beautiful."

She said, "Thank you."

He said, "I'd like to cook for you. Would you come to my cabin tomorrow night?"

Promise said, "I don't know."

He said, "I'm a good cook."

"Well, okay."

"Thank you. I'll see you tomorrow night."

Promise prayed and told God, "I don't like Matthew in that way."

She heard a knock at the door. It was Joseph. She invited him in.

He said, "My father wants me to propose to Sally. If I don't, he'll sell you. What are we going to do?"

Promise told Joseph that Matthew had asked her over for dinner, and Joseph asked, "What did you say?"

Promise said, "I said yes."

"No! You won't go!"

"I have to or Master Jones would become suspicious."

"I feel I'm living a lie. I don't love Sally." He took Promise's hand. "I love you and have always loved you."

Promise said, "We'll have to do some praying."

That night, Promise dreamed that she and Virginia were sitting under the oak tree and Virginia said, "You will be free, and you will marry Joseph."

Promise said, "I can't. It's against the law."

Virginia said, "God will make a way," and walked away.

Promise sat straight up in bed.

The next night, Matthew had dinner ready for her. Promise walked in the cabin and said, "This is nice."

After dinner, Matthew said, "You would make this cabin beautiful."

Promise said, "Matthew, you're nice, but I don't feel the same way you do."

"Sure you do. You'll just have to get use to me."

"No. I better leave."

Matthew tried to kiss Promise, and she tried to avoid that. She tried to get to the door, but Matthew stood in her way. She pushed him, and he pushed her to the floor. She kicked him and ran out of the cabin crying.

Mary saw that her clothes were ripped and asked Promise what had happened.

Promise cried out, "He tried to kiss me, but nothing happened. I kicked him."

Mary hugged Promise, and Promise went to bed.

Chapter

The next day, Joseph went to his father's den and told him, "I can't propose to Sally. I don't love her."

Master Jones said, "What about Promise?"

"I can't live a lie for you. This deception will hurt Sally and me. Promise has helped this family, and she is being used for God. Do you still want to sell her?"

Master Jones got up from his desk. "No, we'll keep Promise. Do what makes you happy." He hugged Joseph, and Joseph left the den.

That night, Promise and Joseph held service in the barn for the slaves. Joseph preached that night; he held his Bible up and said, "Jesus came into this world to bring life. He lived a righteous life." During the service, the people were shouting, and Promise sang.

Promise and Joseph prayed for the people after the service. Matthew walked up to Promise and Joseph and said, "I'm sorry for my behavior the other night. I hope you find it in your heart to forgive me."

Promise hugged Matthew and said, "Yes I do. I hope you'll find the person who will have the same feelings for you."

Matthew walked out of the barn.

Joseph told Promise what had happened with Master Jones and the fact he would not marry Sally. He said Sally was coming over later tonight and he would break things off with her.

Promise said, "Wow! Master Jones said he was not going to sell me?"

Before Joseph could say anything, Sally walked into the barn and said hello to Promise. Promise said hello to her and said, "I'm going back to the cabin," She left the barn.

Sally hugged Joseph, and Joseph said, "I have to talk with you. I don't know how you're going to take this. You're a beautiful woman, and any man would be proud to marry you. But I don't love you. I'm breaking things off."

Sally was in tears. "No! I love you!" She tried to take Joseph's hand.

He said, "Sorry," and pulled his hand away.

Sally said, "It's Promise, isn't it?" She ran crying to the porch.

Master Jones heard her and came out. She told him that they had broken up.

He gave her some brandy and said, "I tried to talk with my son, but he won't listen."

He gave her some more brandy, and they walked to the barn. Sally started to kiss Master Jones, who kissed her back and then closed the barn door.

The next morning, their clothes were all over the barn. Sally asked, "What happened?" Master Jones said, "I'm not sorry it happened. I want to keep seeing you."

Sally said, "Let's get dressed. We'll talk about this."

Chapter

The next night, Joseph visited Promise in the cabin. Mary was asleep in the bedroom. Joseph said to Promise, "I have something to ask you." He knelt. "You are my friend and my prayer partner, and I love you." He opened a box. "Will you marry me?"

"This is wrong. We could get killed, Joseph!"

"I love you." He put the ring on Promise's finger. "This is Virginia's ring."

She looked at the ring and said yes to his proposal; she kissed him.

Mary came out and asked what was going on. Joseph told Mary that he loved Promise and wanted her hand in marriage. He said he knew a minister who would marry them. Mary said, "This is wrong, but in my spirit, I know God is in this."

Joseph said, "We'll leave tomorrow night. I told my father that I was going out of town to a Bible convention. Promise will accompany me. I will be gone for two days."

The next day, a teary Mary told Promise, "If only if your mother could have lived to see this day. She would have been so proud." Mary handed a Bible to Promise and said, "This was your mom's Bible. Let it comfort and guide you."

Promise hugged Mary and left the cabin. Joseph was waiting for her with the wagon and said, "My father doesn't suspect a thing. The minister's name is Michael, and his wife is Martha. We'll get there in a couple of hours. We'll stay with them."

When they got there, Martha hugged Promise and said, "God bless you! We have to get you ready to marry."

That night, Martha handed her a dress and said, "I got married to Michael in this. Try it on and see if it fits." It was a perfect fit. Promise thanked and hugged Martha.

When Joseph saw her, he said, "You look beautiful."

Promise and Joseph were married by candlelight. Martha prepared a wonderful dinner after which Joseph carried Promise to the bedroom. Promise was laughing. He said, "Promise Elizabeth Jones, you are my wife. I will always love you and protect you." Then Joseph shut the bedroom door.

In the morning, Joseph gave his bride breakfast in bed. Promise asked, "What are we going to do now?"

"We could go to a state where you will be free."

Promise said, "I want to be free, but we have to do God's mission. We have to go back and trust in God."

Joseph said, "I don't want our marriage to be a secret."

She said, "I know, but I have a feeling God will work it out."

Chapter

The next day, Joseph and Promise went home. It was a Sunday, and Joseph preached to the slaves. Promise prayed for them, and healing really went across.

An old woman who could not walk asked Promise and Joseph for prayer, so they prayed for the woman. Promise took her hand, and the woman stood. Promise said, "Walk!"

The woman started walking; she was crying. She said, "I've been bedridden for six months. Master Jones was talking about selling me if I didn't get well. I would have been separated from my kids. Thank you!"

She walked out of the barn with the others, and Master Jones came in and said to Joseph and Promise, "You both are doing a fine job here. Joseph, I want you to take over as pastor. My duties as mayor are too much. Promise will help you pray for the people."

Joseph said, "Wow!"

Master Jones said, "There's one more thing I'll tell you tomorrow night," and went to the house.

Joseph said, "Look at God!"

Promise said, "It's a miracle!" and hugged Joseph.

The next night, Promise was working with Mary to help set up the house, and Matthew was working as Master Jones's butler.

Sally walked in with her father, mother, and older brother. Joseph shook her hand and asked, "What are you doing here?"

Sally said, "You'll see."

Master Jones came into the living room and asked Promise to fill glasses for the guests. He said, "I have big announcement to make. I know it's been only a short time, but I love Sally and want her hand in marriage."

Joseph spit out his drink. "What are you? Out of your mind?"

Master Jones said, "You didn't want her. I do, and I love her." He put a ring on her finger.

Sally's father said, "You have my permission to marry Sally."

Sally hugged Master Jones. Joseph said, "This is a disgrace to Mother's memory!" He walked out of the house.

Sally asked Promise, "Aren't you happy for me? I'll be the lady of the house."

Promise just looked at Sally and left the room.

Later, after the guests had left, Promise was cleaning up. Mary told her, "Go find Joseph. I see you're worried."

Promise went outside and saw Joseph sitting in the tree. She climbed up and sat next to him, and he put his head in her lap and cried. Promise held Joseph. He asked, "Why?"

She said, "I don't know."

"This is a disgrace to my mother's memory."

She said, "We just have to trust God."

JENNIFER JAMES LEWIS

Chapter

The wedding was held a few months later on Master Jones's property. Promise was helping Sally get ready for the wedding. Sally looked in the mirror and said, "I look beautiful! Don't you think?"

Promise said yes, and then Sally's mother came in and said, "You look beautiful!" She hugged her daughter.

Her father walked her down the aisle, and she married Master Jones. Joseph sat up front. After the wedding, there was a big reception by the lake on the property, and many attended.

Master Jones said to Sally's mother and father, "I'll take good care of her."

Sally's father said, "I know you will. Enjoy your day."

Promise went into the kitchen and started to clean up. Sally's brother came in and said, "You're beautiful." Promise thanked him and kept cleaning. Joseph walked in, and Sally's brother told him, "She's beautiful." He winked at Promise and left. Promise looked at Joseph with tears in her eyes and hugged him.

Later that evening, Master Jones and Sally left for their honeymoon.

Promise went to Joseph's bedroom and knocked on his door. She went in and sat next to Joseph. He said, "Well, they're married. At first I was upset because I thought it would disgrace Mother's memory, but a peace fell over me. I know it will be okay."

Promise took his hand and stayed with him that night.

A month later, Promise was assigned to Sally. They went to the doctor in town for Sally's appointment. Promise was in the waiting room when Sally walked out and said, "I'm pregnant! I can't wait to tell Master Jones the good news!"

When they got back and told Master Jones the news, he said, "Wow! Well, you'll make a fine mother. I hope it's a boy."

As Sally got bigger in her pregnancy, Master Jones would make excuses about meetings he had to attend and would be gone for hours. One evening, he was gone all night. The next morning, Sally asked him, "Where were you? I was worried about you."

He said simply, "Out."

"You smell like liquor. You've been with another woman!"

He got in her face. "I'm the man of this house! Don't raise your voice to me. Do you understand?"

Sally said yes, and Master Jones left her to cry. Promise saw Sally was crying and handed her some tissue. Sally said, "Thank you. Your spirit is kind."

The next day was Sunday, and Promise and Joseph started the service. Sally walked in and sat in front of the church. Joseph preached, and when prayer was called, Sally walked up. Promise prayed for her. Sally cried and gave her life to Jesus Christ.

After the service, Sally said to Promise and Joseph, "You are so kind. Thank you."

After Sally left, Promise said to Joseph, "I pray for her. Master Jones is so mean to her. Sometimes, I hear her crying. I feel so sorry for her, Joseph."

One time, Sally was reading the Bible on the porch when her mother and brother visited. She hugged her mother and brother. "I'm so glad to see you!"

They sat, and when Promise walked onto the porch, Sally asked her for lemonade, so Promise went to the kitchen. With tears in her eyes, Sally told her mom and brother, "I have something to tell you."

Master Jones walked out to the porch and said, "Well, what a pleasant surprise." He hugged Sally's mother and shook her brother's hand. He started talking to them while Sally was silent. Promise brought the lemonade out and went back to the kitchen. Sally's brother followed her and said, "My name is Gabriel Lewis, and you're beautiful. Would you get me something to drink?"

Promise gave him some water. Gabriel took Promise's hand and said, "I hope to see you more." Promise walked out of the kitchen quickly and stood in the hall in tears. Then she left the house.

After Gabriel and Sally's mother left, Master Jones told Sally, "You don't tell them anything. We're a happy couple."

"That's not true!"

Master Jones yelled, "You'll listen to me or never see that baby!"

Sally said, "You're mean. I'll leave with the baby after it's born."

He threw a glass at her. "You will stay and be the noble wife." He went inside.

Sally sat down and cried. Matthew heard that, came out, and saw the glass on the porch. He asked, "What's wrong?" Sally just continued crying. He said, "I'll clean up the glass." He handed her some tissue. "I don't like to see you cry. It'll be okay."

Sally put her hand on her tummy and said, "I don't know."

Chapter

When it came time for Sally to have the baby, Mary went to get the doctor. Sally's mother and father came. Joseph started praying with Sally and her parents. Master Jones was there when she had the baby. The doctor said it was girl, but then he said, "The baby's not breathing."

Sally started to cry, and Master Jones went to Promise's cabin and told her, "Please come pray. The baby's not breathing!"

She followed Master Jones to the house. Sally was crying, and the doctor said, "The baby's dead. I am so sorry."

Promise said, "Give me the baby." Master Jones gave the baby, shrouded in a sheet, to Promise, and she started praying for the baby. Joseph came in and prayed with Promise. The baby started to breathe and then cry. Promise gave the baby to Sally. The doctor was shocked; he examined the baby and said, "I can't explain what happened, but it's a miracle. The baby is okay!"

After the doctor left, Sally said, "Thank you, Promise. I will name her Olivia Ann Jones."

Promise said, "I'm glad she's okay."

Promise left for her cabin, and Joseph followed her. She hugged Joseph and said, "I'm glad the baby is okay." She had tears in her eyes. She sat, and Joseph made her some tea. He said, "I love you. I hate that we have to keep our marriage secret. I would love to see you with our child."

Promise said with tears in her eyes, "I know it will happen in God's time."

The next day when Promise went to the house, Mary said, "Sally wants to see you." Promise went to Sally's room, and Sally told her to come in. She said, "I've been mean to you in past. I'm sorry. I feel you should be free. I'll talk to Master Jones about that."

Promise said, "Thank you," and left.

Later that night, Sally told Master Jones, "Promise is a good worker. She helps out at the church with Joseph. Promise preaches and does healing, and her prayer saved our daughter. Our daughter is here because of her. I think she should be free."

"She has helped, but the answer is no," he said.

"You're being selfish."

"My answer is still no."

Sally went to Promise's cabin and stood on the porch. "I tried to talk to Master Jones about your being free, but he said no. I can't believe him!"

"You tried," Promise said. "It's okay. The Lord will work it out."

Sally was crying. "It's not fair. I've really grown up since I got married. I love my daughter. But I had no business marrying him. He's so mean to me. He ignores me and our daughter. He drinks and is always away from the house."

"Trust in the Lord. God sees everything," Promise told her and hugged her.

Master Jones saw that hug. When Sally started to walk back to the house, he told her, "I saw you hugging that woman. You don't do that again!"

"You're so mean!" she responded.

He knocked her to the ground and walked off.

Matthew had seen from the window what had happened to Sally, and he rushed out to help her up and back to the house. He said, "I'll bring you a wet towel for your face," and he went to the kitchen for a wet towel and some water.

Sally said, "Thank you. You've been so kind."

"You're welcome. I'm here to serve."

Sally said, "It's a nice day. The sun is out. Talk to me."

Matthew said, "Ma'am—"

Sally interrupted him. "None of that ma'am stuff. Call me Sally."

They talked on the porch for about an hour. When she heard her baby crying, she said, "My baby calls. I enjoyed our talk. We'll have to do it again."

Sally got up and went into the house.

Chapter

The next day, Sally was on the porch with her newborn when she saw Matthew. She asked, "How are you?" Matthew said he was fine. She called him over, and they were soon talking and laughing.

Mary looked out the window and saw Matthew talking to Sally; she called him in and told him, "Please be careful. You're a good worker. I'd hate to see anything happen to you. Master would get angry and would hurt you or kill you."

Matthew said, "I'm not doing anything but talking, but I hear you."

He went back to the porch to resume talking with Sally.

On Sunday morning, Joseph preached, and Sally sat up front with the baby. People were shouting and standing. When Promise tried to stand, she fainted. By the time she came to, the people had left. Joseph and Sally were standing over her. Sally asked, "Are you okay?" Promise said that she thought so. She tried to stand but couldn't. Sally brought her some water.

"I'll bring you back to the cabin," Joseph said.

When they got there, he laid her in bed. He explained to Mary that she had fainted.

Joseph said, "Rest. I love you. I'll do tonight's service," and he left.

"How do you feel?" Mary asked.

"I feel okay," Promise said.

"Have you been getting sick in the morning?"

"Yes, for a few weeks. I thought it was just a bug, but—"

"I think you're pregnant." She kissed Promise's forehead and left the room.

The next day, Sally was eating breakfast when Master Jones came into the dining room. He said, "Good morning, darling," and kissed her forehead. "Sally, I'm doing pretty well as mayor. The council thinks I should run for governor. I'm thinking about that. And I also think we should try for a son."

"Don't you think we should wait? Our daughter is still kind of young."

"It will look good for us as a couple. Our daughter is now six months old. I'll come to you tonight. The only reason I married you was for you to give me children. We can start trying for more tonight."

He left the room, and Matthew walked in and saw tears in her eyes. "What's wrong?" He handed her a napkin.

"Master Jones just told me he wants more children. I don't love him. The very thought makes me sick, but if I refuse, he'll hurt me."

Matthew looked at Sally, and she looked at him. They kissed. Sally said, "I love my daughter, but I love you too."

"This is wrong, Sally. I could be killed. You're beautiful, but we can't do this."

That night, Master Jones walked into Sally's bedroom. She said, "Darling, I don't feel well. Probably a bug. Can we do this another night?"

"Okay," he said. "I'll go for a walk on the grounds." He grabbed a bottle of brandy and left.

The next night, Sally saw Matthew on the porch of his cabin. She went over to him and said, "I can't stop thinking about you."

Matthew said, "No," and he walked into his cabin. Sally followed him in. He started making tea; his face was turned to the stove. Sally took his hands and said, "I know you feel something for me."

"This is wrong. You're the master's wife, and I'm his butler."

She kissed him, and he kissed her back with tears in his eyes.

He said, "What we're going to do is forbidden. I could get killed."

"We'll run away with the baby to Georgia. That's a free state. I'll divorce Master Jones, and we'll be together."

"It's not that easy. You'll be leaving your family, and I don't have anything to offer you."

"Yes you do, Matthew. Love."

"I do love you, but I'm afraid."

"We'll figure this out," Sally declared.

Chapter

17

The next day, Sally's mother and brother came to visit. Promise served them tea, and when she returned to the kitchen, Gabriel followed her. There was nobody else in the kitchen. Gabriel said, "You're truly beautiful." Promise didn't say anything. Gabriel tried to kiss her, but Promise walked away.

He grabbed her arm and tried to kiss her again. Promise said, "No!"

Sally walked into the kitchen and told Gabriel, "Leave her alone!"

"Why are you worried?" Gabriel asked. "She's just a woman."

Sally walked up to Gabriel. "Leave her alone!"

Gabriel walked out of the kitchen. Promise started to cry, and Sally asked, "Are you okay?"

"Yes, thank you," Promise said, and Sally hugged her and told her to go to her cabin for some rest.

Promise went to her cabin and told Mary how Gabriel had tried to kiss her; she burst into tears.

Mary hugged her and asked, "Did you tell Joseph you were pregnant?"

"No."

"You should."

"I'll tell him tonight."

Late that night, Joseph came to the cabin, looked at Promise, and said, "You don't look well."

Promise told him about Gabriel making a pass at her.

Joseph said, "You need to be free. Let's—"

"That's not an option right now. I must finish my assignment for God. There's something I need to tell you. I'm with child."

"What? I'll be a father?" He picked her up and said, "I love you and our child!"

"What are we going to do?"

"We'll figure it out, Promise."

The next day, Promise was in the kitchen with Joseph, and Sally, standing just outside the kitchen, overheard them talking about her pregnancy. She walked into the kitchen and said, "I heard everything. I won't tell anybody, especially not Master Jones. I'll help you hide your pregnancy. I see the way Joseph looks at you. I know he loves you." Sally hugged Joseph and Promise, and Promise told Sally about their secret marriage. Sally said, "Your secret is safe with me."

The next night, Master Jones was at a meeting with the council. Sally was sitting by the fireplace with her baby in her lap. Matthew walked in and said, "We have to talk. We can't see each other. I've thought about it. I love you, but you're Master Jones's wife."

With tears in her eyes, she put her baby in her crib.

Master Jones came home early and heard them talking as he stood by the door. He heard Sally say, "You're right. I don't want to do this, but—"

Matthew kissed her and said, "Goodbye. I will always love you." Master Jones went to hide in his den. Matthew walked out of the house and back to his cabin.

Sally sat and cried. Master Jones walked into the living room and shut the door. Sally dried her eyes and said, "You're home!"

"I heard the whole conversation, Sally."

"What are you talking about?"

He slapped Sally and said, "You were with Matthew!" He kept on hitting her. The baby started crying, and Sally tried to go to the baby. Master Jones threw her on the couch and had his way with her. When he was done, he walked out of the living room.

The door was open, and Mary saw Sally bloodied and lying on the floor, and she heard the baby crying. She helped Sally to bed. Joseph saw Mary helping Sally, and he tended to the child. Sally was unconscious, and Mary went to get the doctor.

Chapter

Matthew was having tea in his cabin when he heard a knock. "Who is it?"

The door was kicked in, and Master Jones grabbed Matthew. "You'll pay for looking at my wife!" Master Jones started beating Matthew and then dragged him to the barn. Master Jones had three men there. One tied Matthew up and whipped him until blood was all over the barn. Master Jones and the other two men were laughing at Matthew.

They put Matthew in the wagon and hanged him from a tree branch. When Master Jones thought he was dead, he cut the rope and went back to the house.

Sally's mother and father were in the bedroom. Master Jones saw the doctor and asked, "Is she going to be okay?"

The doctor said, "She's unconscious. I don't know. I gave her a shot, and she's resting. I'll check on her tomorrow." The doctor left.

Sally's mom cried out, "My baby! What happened to her?"

Joseph walked into the room, looked at Sally, and also asked, "What happened?"

Master Jones said, "I came home from a meeting and found her lying on the floor."

Joseph said, "You don't know what happened to your own wife?" He walked out of Sally's bedroom in tears and went to Promise's cabin; he told Promise and Mary what had happened to Sally.

Promise said, "I'll go to Sally and pray for her."

She got to the house and went to Sally's bedside. Sally's mother was holding her hand. Master Jones saw Promise and said, "Yes. We could always use prayer."

Sally mother begged Promise, "Please pray for my baby!"

Promise put a Bible on Sally and started praying. All of a sudden, Sally coughed and opened her eyes. Sally's mother, Promise, and then Sally started crying. Master Jones said, "It's a miracle!" and took Sally's hand. Sally pulled her hand back. She told Promise, "Thank you."

Master Jones and Sally's mother sat up with Sally all night. Promise went to the kitchen and made soup.

Sally's mother and father left in the morning. Master Jones said to Sally, "Don't tell what happened or you'll never see this baby." He left the bedroom just as Promise was coming in with the soup. Sally was crying. Promise put the soup down and hugged her. Sally told Promise that Master Jones had beaten her and had his way with her. Promise was shocked.

Joseph walked in the room, and Promise told Joseph about Sally and Matthew. Mary walked into Sally's bedroom, and Joseph told her, "I'll take Promise and try to find Matthew."

Joseph and Promise took the wagon and went to find Matthew. They found him on the ground two miles down the road. Joseph saw that Matthew was breathing and said, "There's a barn behind the church. Let's take him there."

Joseph and Promise did. Matthew was covered in blood. Promise cleaned him up. Matthew was still unconscious. Promise started praying over Matthew, and he started to moan and groan. Joseph sent Promise back to the house so the master wouldn't become suspicious. He sat with Matthew.

The next day, the doctor came to check on Sally. He told Master Jones and Promise, "She will recover, but she needs plenty of rest."

Master Jones said, "I'm glad she'll be okay," and he kissed her forehead.

Promise sat with Sally, who was half-asleep. Sally asked, "Is Matthew dead?" Promise did not say anything at first, but then she said no.

Joseph came into Sally's bedroom and asked, "What did Master Jones do to you?" In tears, Sally told him everything. Joseph said, "I'm so sorry. I'll help you and the baby leave him and get to a safe place. We'll wait until you're strong enough to travel." Sally thanked Joseph for that.

Sally got stronger over the next couple of months. One Sunday, she came to church with her baby. Sally smiled when Joseph preached about new beginnings.

After the service, Sally thanked Joseph and Promise for all their help. Sally put her hand on Promise's stomach and said, "Wow! Your baby is getting bigger."

Promise said, "Yes, and it should be here any day."

Joseph told Sally, "Come to the barn. I want to show you something."

Sally followed Joseph and Promise to the barn and saw Matthew. She hugged him tightly. Matthew cried and hugged her back.

Joseph gave Sally a document and said, "These are your divorce papers. I know a lawyer. All you have to do is sign them. Master Jones does not have to know you're divorcing him." Sally hugged him, and Joseph said, "Next Sunday, come to church with your baby. You'll leave to Canada with Matthew."

Matthew thanked Promise and Joseph, and Sally signed the divorce papers.

That night, Promise said to Mary, "This is it. The baby's coming. Get Joseph!"

Mary went for Joseph. When he arrived, Promise was pushing. Mary helped Promise have the baby as Joseph held her hand. Mary said, "It's a boy! What are you going to name him?"

Promise said, "David. He will be special." Mary gave the baby to Joseph, who said, "I have a son!" and kissed him.

The next morning, Sally came down to the cabin and hugged Promise. "How do you feel?"

Promise said, "Wonderful!" She gave her baby to Sally, who said, "I told Master Jones you were sick, and he gave you a couple of days off."

On Sunday, Sally and the baby went to church very early. Master Jones had not come home the night before. Matthew came in through the back door and sat next to Sally. Joseph gave them some papers in the otherwise empty church and said, "I had you come early before people came so I could run the plan by you. I arranged for you and Matthew to get to Canada. Matthew's new name will be John. These are his freedom papers."

Matthew had tears in his eyes. He asked Sally, "You're divorced?"

"Yes. He doesn't know."

Matthew said, "I love you, Sally. Will you be my wife?"

Sally said yes and hugged Matthew. Matthew asked Joseph to perform the ceremony. Joseph smiled and performed the marriage ceremony. Sally and Matthew kissed.

A few minutes later, they heard a knock. Joseph said, "Sally and Matthew, this is freedom."

Sally and Matthew got in the wagon with the baby. Joseph said, "This man will take you to the train station. Your train will take you to Canada."

Sally handed a letter to Promise and said, "Please give this to my mother. I love her."

Promise said, "I will."

Joseph gave Matthew some money and said, "God bless you both."

They left. They were free. Promise had tears in her eyes.

After church, Promise and Joseph went back to the house.

In the evening, Joseph was in the living room reading the Bible. Master Jones asked him, "Do you know where Sally is?" When Joseph said no, Master Jones said, "I bet you she's at her mom's house. I'll go there."

Chapter

Sally's mother and father were sitting on the porch when Master Jones arrived. "Hello there. Is my wife here?" Sally's mother said no. Master Jones said, "She never came home from church."

Sally's father said, "Let's go look for her."

The two looked for her all night. All three went to Master Jones's house. Everyone in Orleans parish looked for Sally and the baby for days, but nothing came up. Sally's father and Master Jones went to look for Sally and the baby some more on horseback.

Sally's mother was in tears and holding a Bible when Promise walked onto the porch. Sally asked, "My baby. Where is she?" Promise gave her Sally's letter, which read,

Dear Mama,

I love you and Daddy. I had to leave. The baby and I are fine and safe. Master Jones was very mean to me and the baby. I wanted to let you know this but was sacred for my safety. I will always love you. Someday, we will see each other again.

Love, Sally

Sally's mother told Promise, "Thank you. You saved my baby's life. I won't tell her father."

Weeks went by. Sally and the baby did not turn up. Master Jones was drinking brandy in the den when Joseph walk in. Master Jones said, "I'm going too legally declare Sally and the baby dead."

Joseph said, "I'm sorry."

Promise walked in, and Master Jones said, "I want you to hear this too. It's all my fault. I was mean to her and the baby. I ran around with other women for years. I was even mean to your mother though all she did was love me. Now she's gone and Sally too. Son, I was mean to you too. I'm sorry. Will you ever forgive me?"

Joseph just looked at Promise.

Master Jones said, "Tomorrow is the funeral for Sally and Olivia. Promise, you will sing at the funeral. I better get some rest."

After Master Jones left, Promise said to Joseph, "I feel sorry for him. I don't like secrets."

"I agree with you," he said. "I will pray for direction on what to do. We should not pay back because we are upset with him."

The next day, it seemed that half of New Orleans was there. Many expressed lovely things about Sally, and after the funeral, all the people came to Master Jones's house. There was a lot of food, and Promise was in the kitchen. Sally's mother told Promise, "I miss Sally, but she's getting a second chance at life." Sally's mother hugged Promise and left the kitchen.

JENNIFER JAMES LEWIS

After the people had left, Joseph told Master Jones, "I need to talk to you."

"Yes, my son?"

"I don't know how to tell you this, but Sally is alive. I can't tell you where she is, but she and your daughter are safe."

Master Jones said, "What? I've been feeling so guilty and you knew they were fine?" He left the den with tears in his eyes.

Later that evening, Joseph went outside and looked up. He asked, "What am I going to do?" He dropped to his knees.

Months went by, and Master Jones did not speak to Joseph.

Master Jones was reelected mayor of New Orleans. He met a woman named Dawn Smith. Master Jones really liked her and started to court her. Next thing anyone knew, they were engaged. He announced their engagement at a big party.

Dawn was all smiles at the party, but she had a dark side when she came to the house; she would yell at the staff.

Master Jones walked into the kitchen and told Promise, "I really like her."

Promise said, "Well, it might work."

Master Jones just smiled.

Chapter

One day, Mary was serving tea and cookies to Dawn and her mother on the porch. Master Jones was at a meeting. Dawn said, "Mother, the wedding plans are going as planned. I'll have this whole estate—"

Mary accidently dropped a glass, and Dawn said, "Watch it, clumsy!" Mary picked up the glass and went to the kitchen. Dawn followed Mary and said, "I know you heard what I told my mother. You aren't to tell anyone!"

Mary said, "Yes ma'am."

Later that evening, Mary told Promise as she was holding her baby, "Please pray for Master Jones. Dawn is not a nice woman. She plans to take him for everything he has."

Promise put her baby to bed, and she and Mary got on their knees to pray for Master Jones.

The next day, Dawn overheard Promise telling Joseph what Mary had told her, and she heard Joseph say, "I'll tell Master Jones."

Dawn told Promise, "You couldn't keep your mouth shut. I'll shut it. You and Mary will pay." Dawn pushed Promise down the stairs, and she fell. Dawn went downstairs and went out on the porch. Master Jones was walking by and saw Promise on the floor. He picked her up and took her up to her bedroom, and Dawn followed them. He yelled, "Mary! Get the doctor!"

Mary screamed and ran out to get the doctor. She saw Joseph and told him what had happened. Joseph ran upstairs and saw Promise lying on her bed and Master Jones in tears. Joseph asked, "What happened?"

Master Jones said, "I don't know. I found her lying on the floor. I sent Mary for the doctor. Promise has been a blessing. I don't want anything to happen to her. Dawn, I need to talk to my son. Will you excuse yourself?"

Dawn said, "Of course," and left the room.

Master Jones said to Joseph, "Son, I've been mean and full of hate for years. I treated your mom, Promise, you, and Sally badly. It took her leaving me to get me to look at myself. I didn't like what I saw. I know what you did was to save Sally life. You did right. Will you ever forgive me?"

"Yes I will," Joseph said.

The doctor came and examined Promise. Master Jones and Joseph went downstairs. Dawn was in the kitchen. Mary was with the doctor in case he needed help. Joseph said to Master Jones, "I have something to tell you. I kept it from you, but I feel in my spirit that you should know. Promise is my wife. I married her years ago. Plus you have a grandson, David Avery Jones." Master Jones had tears in his eyes. "I'll have Mary get him. Promise's neighbor watches him while Promise and Mary work. I love her. She's my prayer partner, lover, and friend. She has to get better." Joseph started crying, and Master Jones put his hand on his back to comfort him.

The doctor walked out and said, "She's resting and will recover. I'll come tomorrow to check on her."

JENNIFER JAMES LEWIS

After the doctor left, Master Jones said, "Go be with your wife, my daughter-in-law."

Joseph and Mary sat with Promise. He told her what had happened and that Master Jones knew about their marriage and their baby.

Master Jones walked into Promise's bedroom and sat next to Promise and Joseph. Dawn was downstairs in the den. It was the middle of the night when Promise woke up and asked, "How did I get here?"

"You fell down the steps," Joseph said. "Who did this to you?"

Promise said nothing, but Master Jones said, "Joseph has told me the truth. I love him and you, my daughter-in-law. Tell me who did this to you."

With tears in her eyes, Promise said, "Dawn did. She pushed me down the stairs. I told Joseph what Mary had overheard. Mary heard that Dawn was going to take you for a fool. She was after you for your money."

Master Jones said, "You are my son's wife, the mother of my grandson. You're family. I'll take care of this. I'm setting my slaves free and will offer them jobs if they want to stay here. I'll have your things moved to my son's bedroom and set up a room for my grandson."

Mary brought David in, and Master Jones held his grandson for the first time. "He looks like you, Joseph. You're not my biological son, but I raised you and provided for you. Promise, you are my daughter from Sarah."

Promise said, "I know. Mary told me that years ago. I don't hate you. It starts off with forgiveness. You're my father. You gave me life."

Master Jones said, "If Sarah were here, I'd make things right."

"I know, Father," Promise said.

Master Jones hugged her and said, "I must make this right, I could tell the sheriff what Dawn has done, but he wouldn't do anything. There's still lot of hatred in New Orleans. I'll break my engagement. You rest. I'm going to talk with Dawn."

He went to the den, and Dawn asked, "Is Promise okay?"

"She's resting. How could you deceive me and hurt Promise?"

"What are you talking about?"

"I thought you loved me. You hurt Promise. She told me your plan. You pushed her down the stairs. Your plan didn't work."

"She's a liar!"

"It's over between us, Dawn. Get out of this house."

Dawn said with tears, "You can't do this! I love you."

"It's over."

Dawn put the engagement ring on the desk. "Master Avery, you and your family will pay for hurting my heart!" She left.

Chapter

The next day, Master Jones gave Promise some papers and said, "These are your freedom papers. I set the slaves free. Some will stay and work for me, and some will leave here."

With tears in her eyes, Promise thanked him, and he gave her a book. "Your mother's husband, Charles, is at the Fair Oaks estate down the road. I sold him when I found out that Sarah was pregnant. Let's go down there to see if he's still there."

The two visited the Fair Oaks estate. The owner asked, "Well, Mayor, why are you here?"

Master Jones said, "I sold a man to you by the name of Charles. Is he still here?"

"Why yes. He works in the house."

Master Jones said, "I'd like to buy him back."

"For twice the price you sold him to me."

"I'll pay it."

The owner said, "Well, he's actually not worth it."

But Master Jones paid the price and left with Charles. He told Charles that Sarah had died when Promise was born.

When Charles saw Promise on the porch, he teared up. Promise said, "Father!" and Charles hugged Promise. Joseph introduced himself to Charles. Master Jones gave Charles his freedom papers. Charles had tears in his eyes when he said, "Thank you."

Master Jones smiled and said, "You're part of the family now."

The next Sunday, Joseph, Promise, and Charles were at church. Joseph stood up to preach, and Master Jones walked in and sat up front. Joseph preached a sermon on forgiveness. Then at altar call, Master Jones went up to the altar for prayer with tears in his eyes. Prayers went up for Master Jones, who fell to the floor. When he came around, he laughed and told Promise and Joseph, "I feel at peace. I feel good."

The church had a picnic that day, and there was lots of food. People were eating and the children were playing. Master Joseph looked at the people and said, "Looks like the people are having fun," with a smile. Promise and Mary helped served the people.

Later that day, a man on a horse came by and said, "The Civil War is over. Lincoln just signed the Emancipation Proclamation." Everyone yelled and clapped. Promise said, "Freedom!" and hugged Joseph.

Later that evening, Mary and Promise were sitting on the porch. Promise said, "Who would believe we're free?" with tears in her eyes.

Mary said, "God will give you the desires of your heart. If only Sarah could have seen this day. Promise, she wanted you to be free."

Promise got up and said, "I'm going to check on David and then go to bed." Promise kissed Mary and left her on the porch.

All of a sudden, a sack was put over Mary's head; she was dragged to a wagon. Mary fought her attackers until someone hit her on the head knocking her unconscious.

When she came to, she was in barn with Dawn, who said, "I finally got revenge. You told Promise, and Master Jones broke off my engagement." Mary tried to say something, but Dawn slapped her and said, "You'll never say anything again!"

Mary said, "You don't have to do this."

Dawn put her in the wagon. When the wagon stopped, Mary got out, and Dawn put a rope around her neck and a sack on her head. Dawn said, "Promise is next. I'll get my revenge."

She hanged Mary until she was dead.

The next morning at breakfast, Charles said, "Mary must still be asleep. I'll go upstairs and get her." Charles went to her room and saw that her bed had not been slept in. He ran downstairs and told the others, "Mary didn't sleep in her bed."

Master Jones said, "That's strange. Let's look for her."

Joseph said to Promise, "She probably just went for a walk." He kissed her and went with Master Jones and Charles to look for Mary.

Promise was on the porch with the baby. She saw a vision of Mary smiling and wearing a beautiful white gown. Then the vision disappeared. Promise started crying.

Master Jones, Joseph, and Charles saw her hanging from a tree. Joseph said, "Master Jones! Cut the rope!"

They had tears in their eyes. Master Jones asked, "Who would do this? She had a kind word for everybody. She was a blessing to me."

He covered the body with a sheet he got from the back of the wagon and drove back to the house. Promise was sitting on the porch. She put the baby down and walked to the wagon. Joseph said, "I'm sorry. She's gone."

Promise pulled the sheet back and screamed.

Master Jones helped Promise and the baby into the house.

The next day, they buried Mary.

JENNIFER JAMES LEWIS

Chapter

The next day, Promise walked into the den, and Master Jones was at his desk reading something. He said, "I'm glad you're here. This paper is my will. I never treated you right when you were young. I was a sick and hateful man to you, Virginia, and Joseph. I now know that I really loved her. Sally never loved me, but she tried to be nice. Nonetheless, I was mean to her. Promise, please watch over Olivia if anything happens to me."

Promise said, "You'll be okay," and hugged him.

There was a knock at the door. Promise went to answer it and saw Sally, who hugged Promise. She was pregnant, and Matthew was behind her with Olivia in his arms. They all came in, and Sally told Master Jones, "The war's over. I wanted my daughter to know her father. We got to town the other day."

Master Jones said, "Can you forgive me for the way I treated you and our daughter?"

Sally said yes and hugged Master Jones, who looked at Matthew and said, "You're alive! I regret the way I treated you. Can you forgive me?"

Matthew shook Master Jones's hand.

Joseph came in and saw Sally and Matthew. He said, "I'm glad you're okay." He hugged them.

Promise said, "I'm going to cook a really good dinner," and she went to the kitchen.

Sally said, "I'll help you, Promise."

Master Jones, Joseph, Charles, and Matthew went out to the porch.

Sally told Promise, "You and Joseph saved our lives. My mother and father cried when they saw me, and they accepted Matthew. The baby's due any day."

Promise smiled, and the two laughed and talked as they made dinner.

Sally grabbed her stomach. "I think the baby's coming!"

Promise helped Sally upstairs to the bedroom, and Joseph went for the doctor. When the doctor came, Promise stayed with him as Joseph went to get Sally's parents.

Sally gave birth to a boy she named Matthew Jr.

The next day, Sally, the newborn, and Matthew got in the wagon. Sally said, "I'll be staying with my folks if you need us." She hugged Promise.

On Sunday, Master Jones went to church with Joseph and Promise. Joseph told Master Jones, "I want you to give the sermon."

"I feel led," Master Jones said. "I haven't given a sermon in years."

During the service, after Promise sang "Jesus Loves Me," Joseph announced his father. Master Jones preached with fire; people were shouting and going to the prayer line. They were being slain in the spirit. He spoke about forgiveness.

That night as they were in the dining room, a rock was thrown through the window. Master Jones and Promise ran outside and saw that the barn was on fire. Joseph, Charles, Master Jones, and some other house staff spent all night putting out the fire.

JENNIFER JAMES LEWIS

In the morning, Master Jones told Promise and Joseph, "I want you two and my grandson to go to our vacation home in Virginia."

Promise said, "I won't leave without you," with tears in her eyes.

Master Jones said, "I don't think it's safe here. I would never forgive myself if anything happened to my family. Promise, I feel danger all around here. Please go with Joseph and David. It's safe there. I'll join you when I can get away. I haven't been much of a father, but I want to keep my family safe. Not too many people know about that house. I used to take Virginia there years ago."

The next morning, Promise, Joseph, and David got into the wagon. Charles said, "I'll stay with Master Jones. We'll join you when it's safe."

Master Jones said, "Please wire me, Joseph, when you get there. Promise, take my will and put it in the safe in the house."

Promise said, "Bless you!"

They rode off in the wagon to the Virginia house, which was big, and there was a lake on the property.

Promise sat in the sitting room and said, "I'm worried." She got her Bible and started praying. Joseph went to town to wire Master Jones that they were okay and at the house, and Master Jones got the wire the next day.

That evening, Master Jones heard a noise outside. He went out to the porch, and Dawn snuck up on him and hit him with a rock. She put a bag over his head and put him in the wagon.

In the middle of the night, Charles came downstairs and saw the front door open. He called out Master Jones's name but got no answer. After Charles looked around the property, he went to the sheriff's office in town.

Chapter

The next morning, Master Jones came to and saw Dawn standing over him. They were by a tree. Master Jones was tied up. Dawn said, "You're finally coming to, Sleeping Beauty. Where's Promise? You give her to me and I'll leave you alone."

Master Jones said, "You don't have to do this."

"She took everything! I eliminated Mary, and now Promise is next on my list. They took my happiness. I loved you, and you broke my heart. Where is she?"

Master Jones didn't say anything.

Dawn said, "If you don't tell me what I want, I'll eliminate you, and then Promise will be next. She will come, and when she does, I'll be waiting for her."

Dawn put a rope around his neck and threw it over a branch. "I left a note on your desk." Master Jones had tears in his eyes. Dawn said, "I love you."

She hanged him and left.

In Virginia, Promise said to Joseph, "I'm worried. Are we just going to sit here?"

Joseph said, "I'm worried too. I'll go to New Orleans and check on Charles and Master Jones. You stay here. I'll come back with everybody."

Joseph left for New Orleans, and when he got to the house, he saw the sheriff and Charles in tears. Joseph asked Charles what had happened, and Charles said, "He's dead. I found this note." Joseph read the note and started crying. Charles said, "We found his body down the road."

The sheriff said, "I'm sad. We're investigating the incident. I'm truly sorry for your loss." The sheriff left.

Joseph told Charles, "I don't believe this note. This isn't his handwriting. Someone set him up. There's something strange going on. I'll get to the bottom of this."

Charles said, "I agree. He had too much to live for."

That night, Promise had a vision of Virginia and Master Jones holding hands and smiling. She knew he was gone.

The whole town was at Master Jones's funeral. Sally told Joseph, "I'm so sorry for your loss." She hugged Joseph and left the church. Dawn came up to Joseph and said, "I'm so sorry for your loss. We had our differences, but he was fine man. Where's Promise?"

Joseph simply walked away.

Master Jones's lawyer asked Joseph, "When do you want to do the reading of the will? I think we should do it soon."

"Give me a couple of days," Joseph said.

That evening, Joseph said to Charles, "There's something strange going on. The lawyer seems to be in a hurry to read my father's will. I want you to leave in the morning so you can be with Promise and my son."

Charles asked, "What about you?"

"I'll be along. It's not safe for you."

"I can't leave. I know it's dangerous, but I'll stay and help."

"Okay. I'll wire Promise and tell her what's going on."

Later that evening, Dawn met the lawyer heard in his office and asked him, "Did you talk to Joseph about reading the will?"

He said, "Yes I did."

Dawn said, "Good. Everything's working out well. I don't know where Promise is, but I'll find out."

She kissed the lawyer, who grabbed a bottle of brandy, took Dawn by the hand, and turned off the lights.

Chapter

The lawyer read the will at Master Jones's home. Joseph, Charles, Sally, and her daughter Olivia were there. Dawn walked in, and Joseph asked her, "Why are you here?"

Dawn said, "You'll find out."

The lawyer said, "You are here for the reading of Master Jones's will. It reads, 'I leave my money to Joseph, my son, but if he dies, it goes to Dawn. My property goes to Dawn and the church. Twenty percent of the church goes to Promise. Five percent of my money will go to Olivia. My gold pocket watch, which I love, will go to Charles. If Joseph, Olivia, Promise, and Charles die, everything goes to Dawn.'"

Joseph said, "I can't believe this! Dawn, my father didn't like you. How could this be?"

"That's what he wanted you to think. Master Jones loved me. He secretly kept seeing me."

The lawyer asked, "Where's Promise?" When no one responded, he said,

"When you decide to talk, let me know. I want to help you settle this matter."
The lawyer left.

Dawn said, "Joseph, we have a lot to discuss. When you're ready to talk,
let me know." She left.

Sally told Joseph, "This makes no sense. He broke up with her, but then
he left her almost everything."

Joseph said, "I know. Let's all meet in the den."

Joseph was with Sally, Olivia, and Charles in the den when Matthew came
in. Joseph said, "I sent for Matthew so he can hear what I will say. Promise is
in a safe location. I don't trust Dawn. There's danger all around us. What the
lawyer read was not my father's will. The original is with Promise. Dawn is
not to be trusted. She's up to no good. She'll try to kill us all so she can have
my dad's fortune. Sally, you, Olivia, and Matthew Jr. are to take the train to
Virginia. Charles will go with you. You are to stay with Promise until it's safe.
I'll wire you when it's safe for all of you to return to New Orleans. I must prove
that Dawn is a fraud, and I have a feeling others are involved. Let's pray."

They held hands and prayed through the night.

In the morning, Sally hugged Matthew and cried. Joseph said, "Wire me
when you get to Virginia."

When Sally, the children, and Charles arrived at the house in Virginia,
Promise hugged them all. Promise was teary eyed at the reunion, and Sally
filled her in with everything going on in New Orleans. When she heard about
the problem with the will, Promise got it from the safe and read it: "I leave my
property including the church to Joseph, my son, who I raised to be a man,
and Promise, my daughter. I give Sally a million dollars, and I give ninety
thousand to my daughter, Olivia. When my grandson, David, becomes an
adult, he is to receive sixty thousand dollars. Twenty thousand goes to Charles,

my faithful servant. The rest of my wealth will be split between Joseph and Promise. Virginia would want it to be this way. I love you all. God bless."

Promise put the will back into the safe. Sally said, "I knew that the will with the lawyer was fake. Dawn is out to hurt us all."

Promise said, "I'm worried about Joseph," and she fainted. Charles caught Promise and carried her to the couch. When Promise came to, Sally was holding her hand; she said, "I sent for the doctor. I'm worried about you."

Charles came back with the doctor, who examined Promise and said, "Well, you're pregnant. Get plenty of rest."

After the doctor left, Sally walked in and asked, "What did the doctor say?"

"I'm pregnant!"

Sally hugged Promise, and Charles cheered.

"If only Joseph could hear the news," Promise said.

Sally said, "You'll see him soon."

Charles said, "It's important that we stay safe here. Joseph will contact us when it's safe to return to New Orleans."

Dawn walked into the lawyer's office and kissed him; she said, "Everything's going as planned."

The lawyer asked, "Has Joseph said where Promise is? We must kill them all—Joseph, Promise, Sally, and Olivia. Only then will we have it all."

Dawn said, "I sent someone to Sally's house. Her parents aren't there."

"Where are they?" he asked.

"Joseph is going to the church. Send some people there to burn it down," Dawn said.

The lawyer laughed at that.

Before church, Joseph read Psalm 121:7 and knew the Lord would keep him from all harm. He realized he had to move the service to another location. He told Matthew, "We're going to move services to the barn."

When everyone arrived at the church, Joseph led them to the barn, and everyone got on their knees and prayed; Joseph read Psalm 91.

Chapter

L ater that day, people in white sheets kicked the church door in and set it on fire.

One of the men went to the lawyer and said, "We burned down the church, but nobody was there."

The lawyer asked, "Where are Joseph and Sally? I'll need your services again. I'll let you know."

The lawyer went to Dawn's house and told her, "There was nobody at the church. I had it burned down."

Dawn said, "We must find Joseph!"

After services in the barn, Joseph told Matthew, "I must find out what Dawn is up to."

Matthew said, "I'll go and work for Dawn. She offered me job a while back. I'll tell her that you fired me. She'll hire me, and I'll find out what she's up to."

Joseph said, "No. If they find out, they'll kill you!"

Matthew said with a smile, "They won't."

The next day Matthew went to Dawn's house and told her, "You once offered me a job, and I want to take it. Joseph fired me."

"Can you start today?"

"Yes," he said.

"You'll work as my personal assistant and work in the house."

"Yes ma'am," Matthew said and started to clean the house.

At the end of the day, Dawn told him, "You did a fine job. The house is spotless. You can stay down the road in the servants' quarters. Sundays are your days off. Tomorrow is Sunday, so I'll see you Monday morning."

Early Sunday morning, Matthew met Joseph in the barn and told him he had gotten the job with Dawn.

"Good," Joseph said, "but please be careful with her. I'll be praying for you."

On Sunday afternoon, Joseph went to the church and saw that it had burned down. Dawn was there, and she told him, "I'm so sorry. I know you loved the church. Your father preached at this church. Promise helped out at this church."

Joseph said, "Yes. I'm shocked."

Dawn asked, "Can you come for dinner tomorrow to settle the will? I didn't want to bother you about that before now because I knew you were grieving your father's death."

"Yes I will," Joseph said.

"Good. I'll have the lawyer here. Matthew works for me now. He'll cook us a fine dinner. Have you heard from Promise?"

Joseph said, "No."

"Well, we'll talk tomorrow night about her share in the will."

Chapter

As Matthew was cooking the next evening, the lawyer arrived; Matthew let him in and took his coat. He saw him hug Dawn. He and she went into the living room, and he asked for a drink, so Matthew brought him some brandy.

Dawn told the lawyer, "Joseph is coming tonight to settle the will, but he says he doesn't know where Promise is."

The lawyer said, "The will states that if something happens to Promise, her portion is split between you and Joseph."

Dawn said, "Good. The plan is going well. Matthew, is dinner almost ready?"

Matthew said, "Yes. I cooked chicken and rice smothered in gravy. The vegetable is corn. For dessert, cherry pie, and coffee later."

Dawn said, "Good."

The lawyer kissed Dawn, and Matthew returned to the kitchen.

When Joseph arrived, Matthew served dinner to the three. The lawyer said, "This dinner is very good. Where's Sally? I thought she was coming for dinner."

Joseph said, "She's visiting her parents."

Dawn said, "I went by one day, and there was no answer."

The lawyer asked, "Where are her parents?"

Joseph said, "I'm not sure. I think somewhere in California I heard."

The lawyer said, "Since you haven't heard from Promise, you and Dawn can split her twenty percent share in the church according to the will. I'm sure you'll rebuild the church."

"I'm working on that now," Joseph said. "I have to go to New York on business next week for a few days."

The lawyer said, "You and Dawn can sign the papers in my office when you come back."

Joseph left after dinner and dessert.

The lawyer told Dawn, "Our plan is working out. Before you know it, Joseph will be gone and we can split everything. We'll be wealthy. Then we can get married."

Dawn kissed him, and they went upstairs to the bedroom.

Matthew had heard the whole conversation. After he finished washing the dishes, he went to Joseph's house and told him what he had seen and heard. Matthew told Joseph that they were looking for Sally and her parents to kill them and the same with Promise.

"Just as I thought, those two are up to no good. I'm leaving town tomorrow, and I'll be back a day early with Promise and Sally and the children. I'll stay at Sally's parents' house. I'll tell the sheriff all about this. I'm positive they'll be arrested for fraud."

Matthew said, "Please be careful."

"I will," Joseph said. "Meet me at Sally's house on Sunday."

Chapter

The next morning, Joseph left for Virginia. When he arrived there, Promise gave him a big hug and started crying. Joseph was in tears as well. He said, "My love, I missed you. You and our son were always on my mind."

When Sally and Charles came downstairs, Joseph filled them all in on what Dawn and the lawyer were up to, and Promise showed Joseph the real will.

"It's safe to go back to New Orleans," Joseph said. "We'll stay at Sally's house, and I'll let the sheriff know about our evidence." He explained that Matthew was then working for Dawn and had overheard their plotting.

Promise said, "I have something to tell you. I'm pregnant! I believe three months." Joseph was overjoyed.

The next day, they all left for New Orleans and got to Sally's house late. Promise helped Sally put the children to bed. Matthew came by, and he and Sally embraced.

Matthew told Joseph that he had heard Dawn tell the lawyer that she had hanged Mary and Master Jones. They were both in on that.

The next day, Matthew and Promise went to the sheriff and explained what Dawn was up to. Joseph showed the sheriff the real will. Matthew told the sheriff that there were plans to burn down Master Jones's house to hurt Joseph and collect the insurance money.

"I'll be there to arrest whoever is involved in this plot," the sheriff said.

The next night, five men wearing sheets rode to Master Jones's house. Dawn and the lawyer came a few minutes later and told the men to burn down everything. The lawyer said, "Joseph's inside."

Just then, Joseph came out of the house and asked, "What were you planning on doing?"

The lawyer said, "You won't be here anymore. You'll leave everything to Dawn."

Joseph said, "I don't think so."

The sheriff and his deputies surrounded the house, and Promise came out and said, "Here I am!"

Dawn's eyes got big. The sheriff grabbed her, and a deputy grabbed the lawyer. The other deputies got the five men; and they put them all in the paddy wagon. The sheriff said, "They'll be in court soon."

Dawn told Promise, "I should have killed you long ago!"

Promise said. "I feel sorry for you. I don't hate you. I'll pray for you."

After the sheriff and his deputies left with the criminals, Joseph said, "It's over." He hugged Promise. Sally came out and hugged Matthew.

"Tomorrow, Promise, we'll have services at the old church."

"But it's burned down!" she said.

"God will restore it, and you'll give the service."

"Yes, and it will be called restoration," she said.

They all went into the house.

Chapter

Early Sunday morning, Promise and Joseph went to the church. Promise said, "This was really burned down. But God will restore it. We'll have church by the lake."

There was a big turnout for the service. Joseph started with a prayer, and he said, "Even though the church is burned down, it can be rebuilt. We're a family. The people are a church, not a building. As long as we have Jesus, we have all we need."

The people cheered. Sally sang "Wade in the Water," and Promise preached restoration. The people were moved; they shouted and went up for prayer. After the service, everyone enjoyed a picnic.

In the months that followed, all the church members helped rebuild the church, and when the day came for the first service in the new church, Promise told Joseph, "I found a flag in the attic at the house. Let's use it at the church."

Promise and Joseph hung the flag in front of the church. Joseph said, "This is the beginning of restoration."

Matthew was installed as pastor. Joseph was a man of God who loved Jesus and me.

EPILOGUE

Rachael said, "That was a good story. Mommy, you better get some rest."

Promise closed her eyes holding Joseph's picture and went to sleep. All the children left the bedroom except Rachael, who sat by her bed and fell asleep.

Promise woke up in the middle of the night. Rachael was asleep in the chair next to her. Promise said, "I love you and all my children and grandchildren. I had a good life. Jesus has been good to me."

Promise took Rachael's hand and said, "It's time for me to go home." She closed her eyes.

A few minutes later, Rachael woke up and tried to wake up Promise but could not. She screamed, and all the children and grandchildren came into the room. With tears in her eyes, Rachael said, "She's gone home." Rachael pulled the sheet over her and spoke Psalm 23 over her.

They had the funeral at the church, and many attended it. David, who was pastor then, performed the service.

The next day, as Rachael was cleaning up Promise's room, she said, "I miss you, Mommy." She had a vision of Promise, who was smiling. Rachael smiled and opened a drawer. She found a diary and opened it. It was titled *Freedom*. Rachael started reading it.

Printed in the United States
by Baker & Taylor Publisher Services

Printed in the United States
By Bookmasters